MY FIRST DEAL PLAYBOOK

ZACK CHILDRESS

www.REISuccessAcademy.com

DISCLAIMER

'This publication is intended to provide accurate and authoritative information with regard to the subject matter covered. It is offered with the understanding that neither the publisher nor the author is engaged in rendering legal, tax or other professional services. If legal, tax or other expert assistance is required, the services of a competent professional should be sought.'

This Material is Not a Substitute for Legal Advice.

While this information has been carefully edited and updated to accurately reflect the laws and local and state guidelines, this is a field that can change quickly. Statutory provisions and legal rules are constantly being changed, revised, and/or interpreted. Readers must use caution before utilizing the information and practices contained within this publication. **This information is not a substitute for expert advice and careful diligence. It is for instructional purposes only.**

This publication is covered under the protection provided by the copyright laws of the United States (title 17, U.S. Code). It is illegal for anyone to violate any of the rights and protection provided by copyright law. Any unauthorized reproduction of this publication or its sections (in whole or in part) will be considered a direct violation of copyright protection and shall be punished to the fullest extent under the law.

Table of Contents

Here's Your
FREE BONUS
($497 Value)

Claim Your Free One-on-One Strategy Session Here:

REISuccessAcademy.com/bonus

or

Call and Request your Free Strategy Session at:
707-310-8113

CHAPTER 1

HOW IT ALL STARTED

"I cheated on my fears, broke up with my doubts, got engaged to my faith, and now I'm marrying my dreams." –Unknown

Congratulations! You have made a choice to gain pertinent information guiding you to a resource that could benefit you, your family and your life. This dynamic new direction is in real estate. A life in real estate has changed millions of lives and I'm sure it will change yours as well.

The question always comes up: why should I read this book? Why should I start looking into real estate investing in the first place? I can reasonably assume that you desire to find an avenue to change your life, to make more money, to have a better lifestyle for you and your family, take more vacations or perhaps to move away from a two-income household and live comfortably on one revenue stream.

Possibly, you are just looking to improve your quality of life. You do not want to work forty-plus hours a week or you have a horrible boss. You have been putting in your valuable time at an office or job site, and there is no longer any real gratification attached to what you are doing.

You are looking for a rewarding avenue; a really engaging path with genuine training, an authentic team with the right support to really help guide you to real success. That success can come from real estate. Furthermore, the practical experience you will gain in real estate can open so many other doors for you to really increase your knowledge and skills in your journey to live a better life. That is how it all happened for me!

Fifteen years ago, I was struggling. I was down on my luck. I had lost a job, and I was facing bankruptcy. I had credit cards companies and collection agencies constantly calling me. Life circumstances had me down. That is why I will never forget the first time I was introduced to real estate.

I was under the impression that you had to have a license or that you had to work with an agent. I believed that great credit was an absolute necessity or that a huge bank account was a must. I thought it was only for the rich. Well, I was wrong. It is not for the rich. It is for the hungry!

It is for the ones who are willing to reach out and change their lives. It is for the ones who are willing to push the boundaries in which they are going, and to not just accept life for what it has been. I discovered these truths and I really created a better life for myself.

That passionate desire to grow myself, my life, and my financial well-being led me down the path to seek information about real estate investing. I believe this same desire is why you are reading this book now.

See, I wanted to really understand what others knew that I had been missing. I had never been taught a strong financial literacy or this type of real estate investing in school. No one in my circle of acquaintances nor in my family guided me in anything other than the old-fashioned ideal of working hard day in and day out. They lived their 40 hour a week career path and never reached out for a greater type of growth in themselves.

A new means of financial freedom and mastery was beyond their vision. Like so many millions, they accepted the status quo of their life. I was coming to realize "that life" was just not for me. I knew I wanted more, and I acknowledged that real estate was the way for me to get it done.

So, I started down that exciting path; like you are doing here today. I began seeking information through reading and studying everything I could get my hands on. Also, I took direction from others with the knowledge I wanted because I was coachable. I can tell you are coachable too or you would not be reading this book.

I knew that there was a massive amount of information in the marketplace on real estate investing; so much so that anyone could get lost in that information. Not that the information was bad, the volume of it just seemed overwhelming. I needed to focus on a very fine-tuned path that I could carry out and master.

That took a while to unfold, but I was lucky enough to find a coach. I found a mentor who had been where I wanted to go, and was willing to help me get to that point.

That led me into my real estate adventure! It is a path that I would have never dreamed would have grown into what it is today. It led me to success in all aspects of my life. In the beginning, I was broke. I had no money, I had bad credit, but I started realizing that there were multiple ways to invest in real estate.

I will come back to those ways in-depth a bit later, but the very first method I used was a strategy called "Wholesaling." Through wholesaling, I was able to build a very quick business making: $10,000, $15,000, $20,000 even $30,000 off of real estate that I never had to buy. Another name for this method is "Assignment of Contract."

Now that is not the only strategy I have stuck with over the years because there are multiple levels; it is really a tier one beginning level strategy. However, it is an entry-level strategy that allows someone to get started in real estate even if they do not have all the resources that others might have.

Through this, I was able to build my real estate business. I was able to create more deals and grow my capital for future investments and for myself. From this entry platform, I was able to move into greater strategies; eventually utilizing a "Buy and Hold" real estate approach which generates a lot of cash flow for myself. Through the "Buy and Hold" method, I own houses, apartment complexes, commercial buildings, warehouse buildings, strip malls and land development deals; even flipping retail estate for very large checks.

That is really what real estate investing is all about. It is starting with point A and never taking your eyes off the end results.

But most people will never venture this far because it does take some work. It takes time. It takes commitment and the ability to be coachable, and receive and utilize information. You see, this is a point in your journey where you have to decide if you are going to dig deeper.

By continuing along your current road, will that grant you the ability to live life on your terms? That is how it happened for me. Now obviously, there is more to the story, but I want to get you started with a testimonial of my own success. Learning how to employ the lessons of real estate investing led me to a life that I live today. Among other things, I get to share my story and teach others how to reach success in their life.

The course I will impart is the same program I use to buy and own real estate from California to Florida. It has led me to a life where I get to travel and spend time with my kids. I get to take them to school and pick them up. I am a coach for their baseball team and I am a youth minister in my church. I have a life that allows me to really be present in my children's lives.

I live the life that I want and I am not bogged down by debt. I am not bound to a schedule of working for others 8, 10, 12 hours a day. The program I will share with you has given me freedom. It has given me a lifestyle that I have always wanted and I am thankful for it. I am thankful also for all the hard times I went through.

I am thankful for not ever giving up. I am thankful for staying committed to my dreams and my goals, and I am thankful that I was smart enough and humble enough to be coachable, and to find a mentor to help me grow up.

With that said, I hope you enjoy the rest of this book. I hope you apply this information in your life, and I really truly hope that you are sincere about this journey that you are about to embark upon.

JOEL ST. PIERRE

From the moment I met Joel, I knew he was going to make it; however, trying to help he see it was quite a challenge. He hired me as a consultant in his business. He really didn't have much experience. His job was an auditor. Naturally, he questioned everything.

You might also have reservations about the process or in yourself, but as I told Joel, "Give me twelve months and I will have you retired from your job." He trusted the process, believed in me, and believed that I could help him. Once he believed, he didn't question anything I told him to do which made him coachable, and within that twelve months, not only replaced his income but well exceeded it.

I remember the day he left his long-term job. He now makes a very comfortable living while he dedicates as much as time as he wants to his family.

CHAPTER 2

WHY REAL ESTATE?

"Success in real estate starts with you believing you are worthy of it." – Matthew Ferrara

In starting this journey, you really need to think about where you are headed and why real estate is the opportunity you have been looking for. If you are looking for extra income, you could do a lot of things, right? You could get a part-time job.

You could drive for Uber. You could deliver pizzas. You could start an online business. There are so many things you could do, but at the end of the day, you and I both know that those options are not really viable. You are here for a reason.

Somewhere along your journey you heard just enough about real estate investing to peak your interest. Perhaps someone has educated you a little bit about the potential in real estate. You are probably aware of the tremendous benefits available through real estate but you just have not figured out how to really strike gold with it. Maybe you are not even sure how to get started.

Let me just tell you this, millions of dollars can be made with real estate investing and there is no reason why you cannot be one of those people, like myself, who make millions of dollars in real estate. You are really no different than I am.

Maybe you are starting in similar circumstances that I faced when I started my journey. Perhaps one day we will meet at either one of our events or our two-day immersion seminars and share stories of our struggles and successes. I think sharing stories helps people relate which is why I want to share a quick story that will help you understand how powerful real estate can be.

From my early exposure, I knew real estate was the way for me. I knew it beyond a shadow of a doubt. I believed I was supposed to be in real estate investing. Thus motivated, I started finding my way.

I really did not realize how quickly you could make a million dollars in real estate when you know all the different strategies of investing. I learned how to have income occurring from different angles or types of real estate; thus, building a substantial lifestyle for myself from real estate investing.

It was so easy to get started. It is probably one of the easiest businesses in the world to get off the ground; so much easier than a franchise. In some franchises, you might spend one hundred thousand, four hundred thousand, or even a million dollars to get a franchise started. Most franchises do not even become profitable for months or years following startup.

However, in real estate, you can make money in as little as seven days. Even newcomers who are just getting started, if you follow the simple process I will lay out for you in this book, you could be making good money within 30 days.

Understand the power of that type of new business. We are not talking a few hundred dollars of profit. We are talking, in many cases, anywhere from $20,000 to $30,000 in average profits on your first real estate transaction!

Think about that. If you conducted only ten such transactions a year, you could be making $200,000 to $300,000 annually! Now, if you really ramp that up and start to expand upon the minimum, you could be making a million dollars a year in real estate. The beauty of it is, it is not just a straight-line process.

There are so many different ways that you can make money in real estate from quick flipping contracts to creative investing in seller finance deals - fix and flips also. What I feel are that paramount tactics are the buy and hold strategies. They all come with advantages. They all have different taxable benefits, profitable benefits, and you gain the sole profits by being your own employer.

You literally own your personal real estate investing business. It is easy once you understand exactly what you need to do, and how you need to achieve your goals.

Another thing that I want you to understand about real estate is that it is all about timing. We are in the best market we have seen in years. You, my friend, need to know how to execute on that.

You see, whether a market goes up or a market goes down, it is really irrelevant if you have been trained by the right coach to show you how to profit in every market cycle. Good money can be made in real estate investing whichever direction the market is moving.

One thing I can tell you, of which you are probably aware, is that real estate has always gone up in value. Twenty years ago, you could have bought my house for $150,000. Now, the same property would go for somewhere around $350,000. Real estate, in the long-term aspect of things, always has the best benefits for you.

Additionally, when it comes to your taxes, depreciation and taxable advantages that you gain and the write-offs allowed are a whirlwind of opportunities; not only to make more money, but also to keep more money than you can believe. Ultimately, that is why you are here. You want to live the cash flow lifestyle!

This cash flow lifestyle is the standard of living that helps you build your future. It is the lifestyle where you have now acquired more rental properties that produce enough cash flow to replace your income, and allow you to move on and live the life that you want. Your investments generate more investments and profits grow. This was a big epiphany for me when I first started out because I never dared to dream I would seriously get into cash flow properties.

This did not seem possible because my current situation had me so far down. I had bad credit. I did not have a lot of money. So, I just focused on tier one wholesaling. It was a beginning, but that was a huge mistake I was making, and it was pointed out to me by my very first mentor. I made a start but I was not pushing myself to reach higher goals.

This coach really invested the time to help me understand what I was doing right, but also what I was doing wrong. A lot of times when we are starting out on a new venture, we get so busy just thinking about what we have to do.

We often fail to realize the direction we are going, and what we ultimately should be doing to progress. When we have some success, it is natural to pause at that plateau. This is what my coach did for me. He sat me down, pointed out the obvious, and gave me a plan of action. Not only that, he led me down a journey in which I realized that I always need to be focusing on the cash flow.

That is the same way I will mentor you. As we go through the rest of this book together, continuously focus on your monthly cash flow desire, and never take your eyes off that goal. That is ultimately the secret to how you will become successful in investing. Instead of chasing the deals, start chasing the future of the potential cash flow lifestyle. Is that not why everybody wants to be a real estate investor?

No one wants to follow this path just to say, "Oh, I want to go out and buy houses, and do all the work on them all day painting and hammering and sawing and cutting." You do not have to do all that work, and I will show you how that is possible.

Everyone wants to get into real estate for the tremendous benefits involved. Benefits like the ability to rent properties out and make real estate your business, create massive checks of cash flow every single month so that you can start to live in that $10,000, $15,000, $20,000 a month cash flow lifestyle.

Your life changes when you start to understand the power of growing and expanding your energies and approaches. None of that would have become a reality for me if I never would have listened to my coach and been open to being coachable when that process started. Therefore, I encourage you to think about why real estate is right for you. Think about why you should be in real estate and the benefits it is going bring you, your family and your extended family. I just know that you are on a journey that is going change everything for you.

CAROLYN HARMON

Carolyn's story is one of many I could tell you. She is another one that had to overcome her reservations, and she had to find faith in me and the process.

After only three phone calls working with Carolyn, we locked up a deal for her to make a $15,000 assignment fee on a wholesale deal.

We have also sniffed out a few more deals. Carolyn is in the New Jersey market, and she is contracting deals in Missouri, Birmingham, and Mobile. She is making it happen, and you can do this too.

There are so many students just like Carolyn. The only difference is that Carolyn put aside her fears, reservations, and negative thoughts and did exactly what we told her to do. She is making it happen. Are you ready to make it happen? The further you push out your start date, the further you push out your success date.

CHAPTER 3

WHAT IS THE BEST INVESTING STRATEGY FOR YOU?

"Don't do what others are doing in hopes of success. Find your own path to success." - Zack Childress

Hopefully by this point, you are starting to get a very clear understanding that real estate investing is more than buying a rental property or working with fix and flip properties. There are a lot of different avenues for you to explore and to think about.

You really need to be thoughtful about how you start in this journey. I say that because I have seen a lot of people getting the wrong support or the wrong training.

They jump into real estate trying to do a strategy of investing they have just heard about or believe will soar their business immediately. However, it does not work for their current situation or their financial state of affairs. Perhaps it is just a bad strategy for them to start with.

Unfortunately, what happens is that it kills their momentum. It is like cutting their Achilles heel. They cannot walk, and they have to run a marathon. Situations like this literally will stop you from ever truly starting a rewarding journey in real estate investing.

I know you are excited. You are all fired up, but you need to slow down a little bit and take stock in your current situation.

What do you have access to? Do you have banks that you can work with? Do you have relationships with lenders that you know would fund your deals? Do you have people that you can borrow money from as a private investor? Do you have relationships with hard money lenders that provide funds based on an asset-based lending? Do you have access to some or all of that?

If you do not have access to any of those tools, then you need to start thinking about other ways to get into real estate. There are other methods through which you can create the opportunity you are looking for.

Do you have a need for immediate cash right now? Do you have a need for consistent cash flow coming in every month? Examining your resources, needs, and assets will allow you to pick the right strategies to launch your real estate investment business.

In the next chapter, I am going to talk about these strategies with you. Afterwards, you will get a very clear understanding of what the different paths are all about. The benefit is that once you understand the strategies, then you know where you fit in. You will know where to get started and how to move through the process of building your real estate investing business.

The beauty of these different paths are that they all have benefits. Each strategy has advantages depending on your needs. Let us say you have really bad credit and you do not really have a whole lot of capital. Well, 'Wholesaling' might be what you are looking for; especially if you have a need to create $5,000, $10,000, $15,000 along the way!

Perhaps you are the person that has bad credit and perhaps you might have only a little bit of income or no income at all but you want to subsidize your living. You need an extra $1,000 or $1,500 a month to really stabilize your lifestyle. This might be a creative investing strategy where you do not have to borrow money from a bank and you can control a property through seller financing that allows you to rent it out.

In doing so, you can create the cash flow from that property without ever having to buy that piece of real estate! That is the beauty of real estate. It is always about you. What do you need? What do you want?

Pinpoint your needs and wants. Pinpoint your assets and resources, and we can identify the right strategy for you. The best advice my coach ever gave me was *"Stop chasing real estate and start figuring out what you need, and then let real estate fill that need!"*

Perhaps you have a very good job making great money, and you have good credit. If that is the case, why waste time with other approaches? Why not go right after rental properties? Let's build cash flow through long-term assets where you gain the benefits of having continuing real estate possessions with all the tax advantages that it brings to you.

Possibly, you have a great job and an exceptional credit score, and a little bit of money in the bank; perhaps $10,000, $20,000 or $30,000. But, you want to build up more capital and focus on running rental properties.

Well, fix and flip properties might be a good thing to consider! You might be asking how do we really do that? Do the repairs yourself? Hire a contractor? How does someone pick the right contractor anyway? How would you determine the value?

Have no worries. We are going to talk about all of that in this playbook.

So, with that said, just remember one thing, do not daydream. This business has a way of taking the most brilliant people and changing their whole mindset. They believe they are building and growing an enterprise because they get fixated on a strategy that they want so bad but they might not have the skill sets.

They might not have any guidance or know how to proceed after a certain point. Consequently, they get pigeonholed and they keep doing the same thing over and over expecting different results; that is the definition of insanity.

Do not be a daydreamer. Be logical about this. Think hard about where you are and what you want to do with this magnificent opportunity. Think hard about what you actually have the ability to do. I meet people all the time that are brand new to real estate investing. They have never conducted a deal before, they do not have much credit, or they do not have a whole lot of money.

These people will come up to me and tell me that they are about to go out and start buying thousand-unit apartment buildings and they are going to put these deals together and make a million dollars a year. I do not ever want to discourage anyone from chasing their dreams, but I am always blown away at how unrealistic that goal is.

That is the goal that we set at an end date. The ultimate goal we want to get to, but we have got to build stepping stones to get there. I encourage you to not be a daydreamer, and to think logically about your entry into real estate investing.

SHIRLEY FALCON

Shirley is one of my favorite students of all time. It is very rare that I get a student that is as determined and immediately trusting of everything I tell her to do.

Because she was so motivated and trusting, it made her road to business success that much faster. Shirley had challenges big time in her market. It wasn't a market that she could reach her goals. She was nervous to look at outside markets, but she trusted my knowledge and experience.

After we did some market segmentation in other markets, Shirley was able to lock up a very profitable 4-plex and tri-plex. The tri-plex is a 44% COCR! The 4-plex is 49% COCR!

These deals are out there. You just have to get the right help and support to get them. Shirley is going to double her income within two years with just these two investments. That is what it is all about!

CHAPTER 4

WHAT IS YOUR STRATEGY?

"The only thing worse than being blind is having sight but no vision." –Helen Keller

In the last chapter, we covered the four main types of investing. These four categories are based on your skill sets, your current financial situation and they are based on how quickly you want to get to a cash flow lifestyle.

These four types are: a wholesaling model, a creative financing model, a fix and flip model, or a buy and hold cash flow model. Also, these models work congruently in your growth patterns so you could start at Tier 1 wholesaling and move your way up into a Tier 2, Tier 3, and into the Tier 4 cash flow approach.

One of the biggest mistakes I see people make; a mistake I made early on, is getting started at a lower tier and becoming stuck there. I was fortunate in my early investing career I had coaches in my life to guide me and to lead me down a path of least resistance. These mentors helped me achieve the end result as fast as possible.

That level of coaching has stuck with me throughout my everyday life. My training repeats these lessons in how I help others reach the success that they want. Therefore, let me break this down for you. Tier 1 is wholesaling. Inside wholesaling, there are really six different features to wholesaling; all of which are separately based on the type of deal you are going after.

It will be based on whether the deal has a lot of equity in it or not or whether the property is owned by a bank, or even if it is a commercial piece of real estate. As I just mentioned, there are multiple ways of wholesaling.

What it is really about is the art of using a contract and having the leverage to sell that contract for what is known as an assignment fee to another investor who is looking to buy a property that they could not find on their own. They will choose to buy your contract on the property you have engaged.

This model is really a strategy for helping investors get started in real estate like I did when I did not have the ability to borrow money from a bank and I did not have a large surplus of capital for down payments or fix up cost.

I could not purchase properties outright with cash either. However, this tactic allows you to go out and find great deals, put them under contract, have the rights to assign that contract, and in return, you can get paid for flipping a contract.

The Tier 2 strategy is known as creative financing. This is an approach that allows you to go out and control properties without buying those properties through a terms agreement with the seller that leaves the financing on the property in place. Or perhaps they agree to seller finance the deal to you directly. This gives you the leverage to be able to create rental properties that you control through creative financing.

You do not even need to buy the rental properties. You can rent out dwellings and create cash flow for yourself on a monthly basis to stabilize your life.

Unlike wholesaling in Tier 1 where you can make $5,000, $10,000 or $15,000 per contract you sell, with Tier 2, the creative financing is really about the cash flow. It is about creating $200, $300, $400 a month, every month, per house that you are able to control.

So, if you are able to get ten homes and you are making $300 a door, you have created $36,000 a year for yourself through a passive process.

Tier 3 is a model that I absolutely love. It is known as fix and flips. It is flipping properties. This is where a lot of new people have a bit of a hesitation, but only because they do not have the right guidance.

Having the right coach to help put these deals together to make the money is very important. It is the lack of the information or knowledge that generates fear. And remember, fear only comes from lack of familiarity. Once you gain the know-how, fear goes away.

In the fix and flip strategy, we are able to find properties that need work. We buy those properties, whether through private funding, hard money lending (also known as asset-based lenders), or through a bank. Some people are able to move right into a Tier 3 strategy while other people have to start in Tier 1 and work their way to Tier 3.

In either case, it is a beautiful strategy because through this method, you can start to earn $30,000, $40,000 even $50,000 on a single flip! That is where your game starts to change. When you are bringing in $30,000, $40,000 or $50,000 per property that you flip, you do not need too many of these deals to live an extraordinary life. The sky is the limit! This now leads us to Tier 4.

Tier 4, passive investing, is ultimately the method in which we all want to operate. Here you build long-term wealth through real estate portfolio properties that you can buy and hold and rent out on a long term basis.

Tier 4 is the strategy where you have a good credit score, your job or some type of income stream which gives you the ability to go to a local lender and get them to finance your purchase with a down payment. You now start buying rental properties and building a cash flow portfolio.

A lot of people want to start here, and I do encourage them to start here but only if they have the ability and resources. Unfortunately, a lot of people cannot start here so they have to work their way towards this by doing other strategies to build the cash reserves they will need to qualify for a loan.

In some cases, they just need to build up the cash needed to pay the down payment for these types of loans which can range anywhere from 15% to 25% down. This may not be the place for you to start, but you do not need to wait forever to do this.

A lot of people do not realize that they have the ability to borrow money right now. For whatever reason, they are afraid to go talk to a lender. In their mind, they believe they are going to be rejected. But I promise you, you will never know until you ask.

One of the best things my mentor ever did for me was to push my boundaries. He made me go out and start doing things that I was not comfortable doing. However, in return, it grew my business much faster having someone to support me and push me. Someone that knew the direction I needed to go. He knew that everything was going to be okay.

Also, remember that when you become an expert in all four strategies, you become a transactional engineer. Becoming a transactional engineer opens up multiple streams of profiting from real estate investing. You now become a master real estate investor, and you are able to take deals that you do not necessarily want to buy and wholesale those contracts out and make a profit on them.

You are able to look at deals that do not have a lot of equity in them and contract them through seller financing to create cash flow. You are now able to look at deals that other investors may run from because they are scared. Perhaps the property needs a lot of work, but you are able to buy them, fix them, and sell them for a profit.

Also, you are now in a position to start buying rental properties and apartments, and create good income for your life. You are creating multiple streams of cash flow coming into your business that will allow you to explode the growth of your journey through real estate investing.

Discover the best investment strategy for your personal situation by taking advantage of the free strategy session you have access to with this book.

Visit REISuccessAcademy.com/bonus

OLIN JOHNSON

Olin is another student that went into a virtual market because his market just was not producing the deals for him to reach his goals. We worked with him on a plan to attain highly lucrative rental properties that have a high COCR.

Together, we found a package of duplexes in an amazing area. The seller is burnt out, and ready to cash out and retire. These duplexes are all long-term rented out except one of them. They are in a great part of town on a quiet cul-de-sac. After we ran the numbers, Olin will have a 40% COCR on this packaged duplex deal.

When Olin locks this deal up, we only need four more deals like this for Olin to retire. This is a big thing for him. His job requires him to travel, and stay away from his family for long periods of time. He has huge motivation to make this happen. You can do this too. You just need the right help and support! Get your strategy session today!

CHAPTER 5

FINDING THE BEST DEALS

"There are no secrets to success. It is the result of preparation, hard work, and learning from failure." –
Colin Powell

By now, you should have clear vision of the journey ahead. You are gaining a concrete knowledge base, and can see that real estate is a dynamic path that can lead you into financial freedom if you put in the work.

You have to remember that nothing in life will ever come unless you pursue it. The key is to be willing to do what others will not do so that you can have what others do not have. This is really a keystone in the foundation of understanding your journey.

We have talked in previous chapters about the best investing strategies for you to start, and how those strategies function so that you can now say to yourself with confidence: "I know where I should start in my real estate investing journey." That is a thrilling mental experience when you have reached that place.

I am happy to be a coach, and guide you through in this playbook. This playbook can steer you down that path and help you get to the next level of your business.

What I want you to understand is that there will never be a profit made in real estate until you understand how to find these deals. However, claiming a good deal is not restricted to calling an agent.

There are deals everywhere. I mean literally everywhere. Yet these will only become visible to you once you open your eyes to the opportunities around you.

With real estate, we sometimes wonder what makes a good deal. Perhaps you question how a seller would sell to me at 50 cents on the dollar? Well, a long time ago a mentor of mine told me, *"Zack, stop worrying about what others will and will not do, and start asking for what you want."*

That helped me really understand the concept of going after seller leads. It really made me understand that when someone is in a distressed situation in their life, it does not always come down to the need for money. A lot of times, it just comes down to the need to remove a painful situation in their life.

That could be anything, such as divorce, bankruptcy, foreclosure, or an inherited property that is in a different state. A person may want to off-load a property because they are having to pay taxes on a property that has been passed down to them and they might not have the financial capability to pay.

Sometimes properties need a lot of work and sellers do not have the skill set or the financial ability to make the improvements. The list of reasons why a person is offering real estate at a great price goes on and on and on. These are a few of the possibilities to reflect on when you ask yourself, "Why would a seller offer me a house at 50 cents on the dollar?"

This is the real estate investing mindset you are developing. I understand that you would probably never sell your house at 50 cents on the dollar, but that does not mean others will not. I am living proof that there are lots of deals out there that sellers are willing to propose.

Some people just need to let go of a property and move on to other things. Sometimes, in an extreme case, you can just take over with no money down, nothing upfront to the seller, no money out of your pocket! You just take over with the financing in place. This is the sort of approach we talked about earlier as a Tier 2 strategy.

I want to move you towards a clear understanding of the two types of lead sources which are public leads and private seller leads. Now, let's talk about these two types of seller leads. A public seller lead is someone who works through an agent to sell their property whether it be a single-family, a multi-unit or commercial property.

Often, the seller hires a representative to handle the transaction for them. Of course, these representatives are known as a real estate agent or a real estate broker. That agent or broker will represent that seller, and they tend to take that property straight to the MLS (Multiple Listing Service). When they put the property on the MLS, it becomes a public listed property for everyone, including other agents, to see.

Of course, every other investor or person looking to buy a property can now see that property. The competition level could be very high depending on the property involved. There is a lot of competition on public properties so getting the best deals off the MLS is not always going to be the most advantageous avenue. It all depends on the market cycle, of course.

When I say "market cycle," I want you to understand that the real estate market moves in many different phases. Ultimately, it is always going up, but there are times when it corrects and temporarily comes back down. Prices and demand occasionally level off or cool down, but these will always go back up again.

The direction of the current market has an explicit correlation to the types of deals you are able to acquire off the MLS. As you can see, if the MLS has an abundance of listings, then sellers are competing with each other because there is so much inventory on the market. This, in turn, means the buyer or investor has plenty to choose from, and prices are economical.

Everyone wants to sell so they are willing to reduce their asking price. Now, we have an abundance of inventory to pick from, and can negotiate our offers in a favorable direction. When the market is down, sellers generally have to keep their property on the market longer than average as opposed to when properties are in demand. Likewise, when the market is taking a shift and demand is high, inventory becomes scarce for buyers or investors to purchase.

Competition switches from sellers to buyers. During this occurrence, purchasing is actually more challenging for a buyer to get a good deal off the MLS.

A quick strategy for utilizing this MLS approach would be to find a very good agent. A professional who really knows your market. Someone that understands the local area and comprehends what you are trying to do as a real estate investor.

An agent who is willing to work with you and assist you in getting that first and second deal. A representative who will provide you with comps. Comps are how the After Repaired Value (ARV) of a property in that area is determined - a snap-shot of what the property could be. Agents can provide you with Comps through a CMA report, the Competitive Market Analysis report.

Let me stress that having a good agent is very important for the creation and growth of your business. Even if you stick with private seller leads, you need an agent to help get comps and process the sale.

Moreover, when you are working with that agent, you want to set up some criteria to put in the MLS to bring you deals at will. What I mean are things like first day notification for new property listings that meet your specifications such as a certain area of town, a certain price point that you want to buy, approximate square footage, number of bedrooms or baths, the precise school zoning, and things of that nature.

Another item you want to execute is setting up a criteria to be notified of any property that has been on that market longer than 120 days. Sellers are more motivated to adjust terms the longer their property is on the market.

Finally, you want to set up a criteria with your agent for any item on the MLS that drops in price. By using these criteria, you can see when a seller is getting aggravated. They are now more motivated to sell which is beneficial to you.

These are the criteria you want to establish when working through the MLS. These, and also picking a good agent, will be very beneficial for you. Just keep in mind that we have been discussing public leads to this point which means these are leads that everyone else can see and act on as well.

The second type of lead source is private seller leads. Private seller leads are by far the most important lead source that you will acquire in your business as a real estate investor because they are private sellers.

They have not hired agents. You typically see these as 'For Sale by Owners' (FSBO). There is not a lot of competition looking at this type of lead. Obviously, they are not on the MLS so most people do not know about the property. This gives you the upper hand knowing that you might be one of two or maybe three people that are actually looking at the property. You have a tremendous head start in the negotiation process with a seller lead.

It is also beneficial because you can control the paperwork a lot easier with a For Sale by Owner. You can quote me on this: whoever controls the paperwork, controls the deal. It is the truth.

A For Sale by Owner in which you control the paperwork, offers the option to do the Tier 1 or 'wholesaling' strategy, if you so choose. You might also select to conduct a Tier 2 or creative financing strategy. You could quite possibly take over the property without putting any money on the table.

This gives the real estate investor so much more control, especially the ability to communicate directly with the seller. You can even learn to use a script to identify the pain - why that seller is trying to sell and the reason they would let that property go without making a large amount of profit, or any profit for that matter.

As you can see, private seller leads are by far the number one lead source for your business. It gives you the upper hand and far more control. Ultimately, it gives you the ability to make more profits.

Nevertheless, there are a few considerations when you are setting your sights on private seller leads. One of the easiest places to look, something you can do right now while you are reading this book, is search private seller leads on Craigslist. You can also find sources for them on Zillow and Backpage.

Others will be listed on HotPads and many other sites such as: For Sale by Owner, Will Sell, or FSBO.com. Those are the most popular sites that you can start sourcing and they are all free! You do not have to pay any sort of fee associated with some methods. When looking at private seller leads, there are free methods and there are paid methods.

You do potentially get better leads using paid methods, such things as: ad placement (whether online or offline), some form of direct mail where you are seeking out-of-state owners, equity rich properties, vacant properties, or burned out landlords. Each of these lists are potentially very lucrative for a real estate investor but these are just the tip of the iceberg regarding how you can seek leads.

Another thing to think about is a SEO campaign or a Google AdWords campaign.

Possibilities such as these really help build your business model while generating plenty of leads.

One last thing to consider before we move on is that you should constantly be looking for leads. You need to be building your relationships with people - personal contacts to business contacts - real estate agents and banks. These connections start at your local real estate investors association.

Building your network is a continual job so that everyone knows that you are in the business of buying real estate. Yet again, this creates a lot of lead generation for you.

I will give you an example. At my children's school, I tell everybody (including the teachers and principal), that I buy real estate. About six months after my daughter had started second grade there, the principal came up to me and told me he had an investment property that he no longer wanted and was curious to see if I would buy it.

I gathered all the information from him, looked into the place and ran the numbers, but I realized that the deal was just not for me. However, it could be a great deal for someone else. So, I reached out to another investor I knew and they were indeed interested. That is a fine example of a Tier 1 deal.

I put the property under contract with the rights to assign my contract and I sold that contract to the other investor for an $8,000 assignment fee. That deal came together in less than 10 days. As you can see, just letting people know your professional interest, networking and working deals with others is also an avenue from which you can make quick money.

Think about that; $8,000 in 10 days. That could change someone's life. That is a nice bit of extra money for anyone. You can do this too! As a coach once told me, *"Zack, your limitations are only what you set on yourself, and the lack of education is what prevents you from moving forward."*

I am here to tell you that you can do whatever you choose as long as you put the time and energy in to educate yourself. Get the right training and the right coach or mentor. This is where you really start to grow in your marketing and in your analyzing of transactions. You are now able to receive answers from someone that knows the ins-and-outs of this business. And yes, you have to invest in yourself.

The best thing I ever did in my life was invest in myself. I invested in my education to be a business owner as well as coaching and mentoring. It is how I became a master marketer, and how I was able to build all the different companies that I own.

I share this with you because I want you to know that you are on the right path. At this point, you might start thinking to yourself, "How am I going to get all this done?" You are thinking too much. We just need to create a very specific plan for you that is tailored to your needs, so that you can reach the success that you want.

RICK HORTON

"We've been investing in real estate for a while, all in income properties. Then, I met Zack. I attended one of his 3-day events. While he presented a lot of great information, it was market segmentation that would prove to be of most value. It was this concept that showed us that a property we found would be a great rehab and sell prospect.

We paid $100,000 for this HUD property, determined that a renovation budget of $60k should be adequate and began to work. As happens, we ran across some unexpected expenses, but we still expected to turn a profit. With some additional guidance from Zack all along the way, we continued the project.

In the end, we found the property had a higher ARV than we calculated in the beginning (a very good thing to have happen).

We listed the property on Friday, had two offers on Sunday and sold for $245,000. So, even with our unexpected costs, we pocketed over $50,000 in net profit.

During this project, Zack has been in frequent contact, helping guide us not just in this case, but he's also provided us systems to streamline and strengthen our investing.

Because of Zack, I am sure we will have a prosperous real estate business. In fact, we're so confident that I have just quit my J.O.B. and we are well on our way to financial freedom through real estate."

-Rick Horton

CHAPTER 6

RESEARCHING YOUR DEAL

"Real estate investing is not emotional. Learn how to run your numbers, trust your numbers, believe in the numbers, and you will know if the deal is a deal." - Zack Childress

By this point, you should understand that a lot is going to depend on your ability to pursue great deals. I realize, like most people just starting out, you might get a little nervous. Even experienced investors get anxious at times. However, I am confident that through this knowledge of acquiring great leads, you can find profitable deals.

At some point, the new investor might freeze because they just do not understand what they are looking at. This person does not know if they have a good deal or a bad deal; they do not know if it is high risk or what it might sell for. They do not know what to offer on it.

Obviously, they do not want to lose money on the deal so they hesitate. A key element that turns nervous first-time investors into savvy real estate specialists is that they do all the stuff necessary to acquire good deals, and they listen to their coach. An important role for a coach is to direct them in the process of finding good deals.

So many things might flash through your mind such as: "I have a seller who wants to go through with the transaction, now what do I do?" Well, that is a great concern to have. It is a great position to be in because you are starting to evaluate or research your deals, which means you are moving forward.

You have taken the initiative to get out there and start doing something. Consequently, the worst thing that can ever happen on your journey as a real estate investor is allowing uncertainty to take control and halt you from taking initiative.

That sort of thing happens when you do not have the right support or guidance to encourage and direct you through the process.

If your mental horizon is limited, you will get stuck because you know nothing else. You will never reach beyond your current level until you move out from your comfort zone and ask for help.

However, when you receive and trust in that support, you begin to grow to the next level. You see it can be done, and only then do you start to realize that you are moving in the right direction. Having tangible results is a big shot to your confidence especially when it comes with the right help and support.

You know you are part of a structure that is geared towards your success. Additionally, researching a deal is very repetitive so once you get some experience and you understand the processes you go through, you simply repeat that over and over on every single deal and there is nothing intimidating about that.

You might ask yourself, "Well, once I have a deal, what do I do with it?" Let me clarify a few points. When we say we have a deal, is it a solid agreement, a potential arrangement, or is it just a lead? Clarifying that point helps you by really identifying what type of strategy you are going to implement in the market.

If you are a wholesaler, you are definitely going to make sure that you are getting the deals in the areas where other investors are buying. Closing a deal in desirable areas gains the best opportunity to leverage your new deal to other investors.

If you are using a strategy for creative financing to generate cash flow or perhaps structure a Tier 4 passive cash flow model, then you want to make sure that the deals you are seeking are in areas where you can rent quickly and produce a stable income.

If you are aiming for a Tier 3 strategy model to fix and flip, then you want to make sure that the prospects you are looking at are coming from areas that have a higher percentage of first-time home buyers as opposed to other types of buyers or rental properties.

First of all, know the territory. You need to know the vicinity in which you are targeting very well. By identifying areas that will be profitable for your model, you can target where your leads are coming in.

When you start your research, you can immediately look at the area first and say, "Look, this area or this neighborhood is right in line with the strategy that I want to pursue. This area has 80% of closings from first-time home buyers, and there is only a 10% or 15% of rental properties. There is also a low ratio for foreclosures in this area."

That scenario means it would fit your criteria as a Tier 3 investor. These are some of the initial things to think about when you start looking at locations.

To follow up on this, you want to create what is called a zip code matrix. When I first started out, this was something that my coach showed me and it literally changed my entire approach to real estate investing.

Soon after, my risk management was on par with the potential gains and I knew, before I ever investigated further on a deal, exactly what had to be done to make that deal profitable for me just by the location of the property. It's simply a matter of knowing how to pull the data to create a zip code matrix.

First and foremost, know your target location. Know what strategies work best in your area. Know what is going to be the easiest approach to get deals done in that market.

The second thing that you need to start considering is value. How do we really know a property's value? What could this property sell for in "as is" condition? What could this property sell for if it were fixed up? We refer to that value as ARV which stands for <u>After Repaired Value</u>. ARV helps us identify what we could sell that property for once it has been improved or repaired.

In those cases, we can start running our numbers off the ARV to determine what our offer price should be. This will act as a safety net of sorts so that we make money while we cover all expenses that are going to be incurred in refurbishing that property. Consequently, this is also the starting point of a good Tier 1 wholesaler. It is the point where we can figure out what our investors can pay. Ultimately, we know how much we can charge to sell our contract to another investor.

Therefore, figuring out value is not always as difficult as many people think. It relies on your ability to find similar sold properties in the area in which you are operating, and also making sure that it is of like kind which means same number of bedrooms or bath, approximately same square footage, same exterior look, and things of that nature.

Also, if you can get comparable properties in the same neighborhood, you are doing yourself a world of justice regarding knowledge of potential value. That type of information will also help you determine how quickly and at what price you can sell the property. However, you will learn that asking for a CMA report from an agent is not always helpful.

They might pull properties from streets scattered over many miles or even include properties from other subdivisions entirely. This does not give you the accurate value for the property that you are interested in if you are comparing units in completely different neighborhoods.

From this point, you have to work your numbers backwards. ARV minus 10% which includes your real estate commissions and closing fees or additional fees that you might want to give to the buyer if you are selling.

You might be expected to pay extra closing fees or seller credits. You also have to subtract any fix up costs and any holding costs. Lastly, you must subtract any purchase fees that you might be expected to pay while buying the property. At that point, you want to subtract whatever profits you are interested in making.

In total, these numbers will give you the Max Offer Price or MOP. The MOP is the maximum you can pay while keeping yourself safe in a deal. Always start your offer below the MOP. We will talk about that in the next chapter.

Keep in mind that running your numbers is a repetitive process and numbers do not lie. Remember, this is not an emotional business. This is not about how pretty the houses are. This is strictly a numbers business. This was another fact that my coach taught me years ago - to remove myself from the emotional aspects of the real estate and focus only on the data, the zip code matrix information, and the research and the analysis of the numbers and to only believe in the numbers that I run.

Do not get caught up in how pretty the property is, the desirability of the neighborhood, or what color you are going to paint it. Before all of that, run your numbers. Numbers do not lie!

That lesson was 'hammered' into me from my first coach. If it was not for that coach, I do not know if I would be as successful in real estate as I am today! I owe everything to my coaches for not only showing me the path and keeping me focused and accountable in the business, but also showing me how to grow and how to scale my businesses.

He mentored me in how to really focus on what matters when it comes to the numbers, marketing, negotiations, scripts and communication. He guided me as I took all these tools and leveraged them into a multimillion dollar business.

I share this with you, my friends, because I want you to succeed. I am here to support you when you reach out for help. I am here to assist you!

WALTER RANCHINSKI

Walter has a story that I think would motivate anyone. When Walter came into my program, he was overeager. He wanted things to happen right way, but as a good coach, I had to back him up, and get him to pace himself a little bit. Walter also had some pretty heavy stuff happen in his life. He had someone dear to him pass away, but he had the determination and will to keep pushing forward in his own life.

Today, Walter has found a condo that he can buy for very cheap, and there are only about $15,000 in repairs needed. He already has a buyers list that is heavily interested in condos in this particular area. He is going to fix and flip this one very quickly for a $35,000 profit.

This is what the power of having a coach can do for you too! Walter is making it happen even through troubled times. He is securing lenders in his area that will finance him on demand. That is a beautiful thing to have in your back pocket when great deals come to the table.

This is something that you can do too. The power of a coach to guide, uplift, keep you focused, give you the knowledge, give you the confidence, and get you to the next level in your business is what it is all about.

Take the challenge. Fill out a strategy session application, and submit it to my office so we can get on the phone with you. We need to see where you are currently in your business so that we can guide you to the next level in the fastest way possible.

I say all the time, "I am not your guru. I am your coach. Gurus are here for your money. This is not what I do. I am here to coach you, and guide you to success the fastest way possible." Fill out a strategy session application, and let's get on the phone. I want you to be my next success story!

CHAPTER 7

MAKING OFFERS

"To accomplish great things, we must only act, but also dream; not only plan, but also believe." –Anatole France

Now you are ready for the journey of purchasing real estate, managing real estate, and making money from real estate. It is an incredible feeling that you get when you set out on a journey, or when you set a goal for yourself and you start taking small steps to reach an ultimate goal. Along the way, you periodically stop for a minute to look back and realize how far you have come.

Well, this is one of those points. Reading through this book, you have probably come to the conclusion that this business is absolutely the business for you, and it is not as complicated as you thought it would be. You have come to the conclusion that for any steps in the process that you do not fully understand, you can get coaching.

You can get guidance from a coach that will lead you down the path to that rewarding venture. I commend you for taking that action and for being involved in seeking the life and freedom that real estate investing can offer you.

As you move through this journey of becoming a real estate investor, you realize that you are building processes and putting systems in place to further understand what strategy is the right one for you.

As you have learned, it all comes down to leads. In the previous chapters, you have learned about various types of leads you need to recognize, and where and how to get them. Also, the ability to do research regarding those deals is a fundamental that you have to acquire. Of course, you realize that nothing is going to materialize if you never control a property.

Believe it or not, controlling properties is simply an understanding of which type of paperwork is right to use on that specific piece of property, based on your chosen strategy model.

Obviously, no deal is accomplished unless the seller agrees to sign the contract. This contract can be anything from purchase and sales agreements to LOIs (more on those a little later). As I have said before, you have to be in a mental position to take action to put a property under contract because if you never move past the research stage, you will never make money in real estate.

The only way to make a profit in this business is by putting properties under contract no matter if you want to buy and hold them, rehab them, wholesale them, or position some creative financing on that structure of the deal. None of that will ever become a reality for you unless you move forward and take action in the contract stage of your business.

So, be confident! Be assured that you are making the right decision. If you ran your numbers correctly and you know that you have got a good deal because your offering is below your MOP (Max Offer Price), then you are on the right track. Move forward and take action. To continue your successful beginning, you have to put that property under contract!

This is the point when a lot of people freeze because it is the unknown. It is a process that they have not done before. Too many new real estate investors say, "Oh my goodness, what am I going do if the seller says yes?"

This is why I keep encouraging you to get the support and coaching you need to help grow - not only your confidence - in your business. If the seller does say yes, that would be the best thing that could happen!

Now your business is in play. You are in the game. It is time for you to execute a contract on that property.

No successful sports team has ever accomplished a championship without a coach that pushed them. Even professional athletes are told how to play the game and execute a game plan. Athletes have the skills and potential, but the coach brings out that talent and allows them to explore their internal abilities.

The football or baseball player pushes themselves because they have the reassurance that their coach is knowledgeable and able to develop their full potential. It is similar to our business model when we have coaching. We rely on the expertise of a mentor to guide us. I have been blessed to coach so many people in my time as a real estate investor and educator.

Mentoring and helping new investors find the faith in themselves to explore what they can become in the real estate market has been one of my great passions. When it comes time for that first contract, I encourage you to dig deeper into who you are, and take the action to move forward.

One thing I want to encourage you when getting knowledgeable about contracts is the importance of staying in control. Fortunately, this is easily done when we are working with private seller leads such as For Sale by Owners because we can use our own contracts with our personal clauses and terms as we want them written.

As I told you in the previous chapter, the person who controls the contracts or paperwork controls the deal. Keep this in mind as you move forward.

With individual contracts there are some things to be aware of to keep your paperwork legitimate and the transaction valid. For instance, no contract is fully executed until both parties have signed and monetary exchange has happened.

This is known as "Earnest Money Deposits," and they could range anywhere from $100 to $5,000, depending on the seller. That money has to be written to an Escrow account. To validate your contract, you need to open Escrow. The money deposit will make the contract a lawful agreement.

If you are concerned about the Earnest Money Deposit, you can always put a clause in your contract that simply says, "All earnest money deposits are fully refundable to the buyer whether this transaction closes or not." This little clause keeps you safe. No matter how much capital you put down you can always get it back.

Another helpful article you can add is what we call an "Inspection Clause." An inspection clause typically spans from 7 to 21 days, and gives you the ability to analyze the property, rerun your numbers and determine if any part of the property needs renovation. You have time to see for yourself if any element of the property is outside the scope of work in which you originally ran your numbers.

If you find something that is beyond the scope of what you want to repair or if some other unforeseen factor presents itself, you have the ability to pull out of the contract without worrying about losing your earnest money deposit.

Another thing to consider if you are a Tier 1 investor, is to make sure both parties are in agreement and that the seller is aware of your rights for assigning or selling the contract. Contract Law states, *"All contracts are fully assignable, unless otherwise stated not."*

Still, we want to take it one step further and make sure the seller can acknowledge our intentions. This avoids misunderstanding while building up our professional demeanor. The simple clause states the, *"Buyer reserves the rights to take title in name or entity of choice."* This grants you the ability to close in any name or company name that you choose.

Ultimately, this simple clause allows you to assign your rights to a new buyer who can then go and close in their company name. These are some elements you really want to understand and direct as you conduct your transactions.

Another tip is if you are conducting transactions dealing with buy and holds, there should be some special clauses that state that the contract is contingent on receiving lease agreements, expense reports, and rent rolls on the property.

Through this, you can really understand that the asset and investment is performing like the seller has told you. There are all different types of language that we can put in contracts to give us a safety net. However, do not get too complicated with it. Just keep it simple, and keep it safe.

When you are a brand-new investor looking into real estate and you have never made an offer on a property, you could be thinking about a purchase contract which is a Purchase and Sales Agreement and a LOI (Letter of Intent). I have always taught my new investors to use a LOI. The reason being is it is non-binding.

You could make 1,000 offers using an LOI, and if you got 1,000 sellers to say yes, you are not bound to do anything. It is non-binding. The LOI basically outlines what you want to pay, and what the offer would be contingent upon. If both parties agree to the LOI, you then move forward with a Purchase and Sales Agreement.

If you are brand new to real estate and you are starting to take action, then use a Letter of Intent. LOIs will help you in the process of getting started without unnecessary stress or anxiety. Remember, the letter of intent is non-binding, so you do not really have a deal until you move forward with the Purchase and Sales Agreement. It is a safety net, but you still need to close the deal to make a profit.

There is one other thing I want to clear up in this process. You do not have to use a state-approved contract supplied by real estate agents. If you are buying a property from a For Sale by Owner or a private lead source, you can use a one-page (or multi-page) general Purchase and Sales Agreement to secure your rights to buy that property.

This does not have to be a state-approved contract. If you are using an agent and you are buying properties off the MLS, they will mandate that you use a state-approved contract. The state-approved contracts are there to protect the agent's broker from any litigation and lawsuits for misrepresentation aimed at them.

You will discover that while working with agents there is nothing wrong with state-approved contracts, it is just the legal process which you will have to go through.

Now, let me be very clear on another key point, you do not need to be a licensed real estate agent to be a real estate investor! Once again, you do not need a real estate license. I have been investing for 16 years full-time, and I have never attained a real estate license. I do not need it and neither do you.

To summarize, to be successful in real estate investing, you must take action. Move forward, and take the next step in the process of building your real estate business. This will require you to get comfortable making offers on properties. Use your own contracts when possible so there will be security clauses built in.

Choosing whether to pursue a purchase and sales agreements or an LOI is another consideration. Both have advantages in given situations, but ultimately, you need to choose whether to move forward or stay stuck in a rut.

I encourage you to recognize when you are stuck, and recognize it quickly. Then, you can determine how to move forward. Keep taking the steps and actions to move your business forward.

SCOTT WALTER

"In the beginning, I was all over the place. Zack helped me focus and time block. He slowed me down and gave me expert advice on what I needed to do. The first time I was on the phone with him, I was skeptical. My wife told me to go all in which was exactly what Zack told me to do. He told me that I couldn't do this business and be successful with only one foot in the door.

I was working at a job that I really liked. Unexpectedly, they decided they did not need my position anymore, and they let me go. I didn't freak out about it. I talked to Zack and he told me not to go back to a J.O.B. We worked out a plan to replace my income and then some. That was very hard for me. We, as people, are trained to graduate high school, graduate college, and go work for someone. I did not have the mindset to do anything other than working for someone else.

I had two rentals when I met Zack. Now I have over twelve multi-units, and I have completed over ten flips. Working for yourself has its challenges, but I would not have it any other way. To actually be in my kid's lives, be present, and see their faces light up when I show up to all of their activities has been that freedom that I have always wanted.

My wife called me one day and said she is going to lose her job in three months. I called up Zack and we discussed how I could replace her income. In an hour, we had a plan. I called my wife up, and I told her that we are going to be just fine. Now she is a stay-at-home mom, and we are both enjoying life with each other and our kids. We are leaving our legacy for our kids and our kid's kids!

If you want to get into real estate at any level, call up Zack today. He genuinely wants you to succeed. He is not one of those people who sell you a course, and tell you 'good luck' and you never hear from him again. I have been working directly with him for over three years now. Zack has taught me the 5F Lifestyle, and I am proof that his system works. Thank you, Zack!"

- *Scott Walter*

CHAPTER 8

DO YOU NEED MONEY OR NOT?

"If you always tell yourself you don't have money, you will never have money. Change your mindset, change your life." - Zack Childress

In this chapter, you will have one of the big questions addressed. It is the question about how to finance all these real estate deals. People always say, "Well, Zack, real estate investing sounds great, but you need a lot of money to do it, right? I do not have those kinds of resources." That line of thinking is false! I can assure you, you do not need personal money to get into real estate.

You do not even need great credit or a real estate license to get into real estate. What you do need; however, is a lot of knowledge to maneuver yourself into maximizing great real estate deals.

What you need is the right direction and guidance to close your real estate deals. You should definitely understand your current situation and what you have access to, but there are fundamental strategies to aid you in your journey.

Your business may start with minimal assets, but you do not need access to a fortune or have stellar credit to get underway. Back in Chapter 3, we talked about recognizing the best investing strategy for you to start with. Revisit this concept because you need to have a very clear understanding of your current life and build from that.

Look at your own personal finances. If you do have money or access to banks, then your investing career is just going to be able to start much faster than someone who lacks the funds or a working relationship with a bank. You can move right into cash flow real estate.

However, if you do not have a lot of money laying around or your credit score is less than excellent, then you need to examine the strategies that will grant you the best starting position for your situation. In these circumstances, you may consider Tier 1 wholesaling which does not require money down.

Also, Tier 2 creative financing does not require money to begin. This would be the place for you to start. You can build your network and your capital before moving on to the next strategies. Both Tier 3 and Tier 4 require money up front along with some form of marketing budget if you want to quickly grow your marketing (remember, we talked in Chapter 5 about free methods of marketing).

Therefore, most beginning real estate investors will want to work their way into these levels.

Too many times, new students that I mentor do not execute the simple game plan. They tend to use their lack of funds as an excuse for their life's situation or their limited success in business. "I do not have enough money to achieve X, Y, and Z," they say. "I do not have enough money to get started" or "I do not have enough money to do this."

"I do not have enough money to do that. This will not work for me because I do not have money." The more you tell yourself that you do not have money or that you are living your fullest reality without chance of advancement, the longer you will be stuck in your situation.

Do not believe the incessant idea that just because you do not have personal wealth in your bank account that there are not individuals or companies out there that you can tap into. There are abundant resources all around you that you can attain access.

Numerous types of lenders work with real estate investors; these are what we call "Asset-Based Lenders," and I will fill you in on these a little bit later. I will tell you at this point, they care nothing about your credit, your current job or your bank account balance.

Do not let the fear of money stop you from what you want to accomplish. The fear of finances should not squash your dreams. However, be realistic about your current situation and what strategies will work for you as you start your investments in real estate. Though, if you think Tier 1 wholesaling is the only strategy you can possibly accomplish and the only level you will be successful with, I would tell you that you are wrong.

You can mix and match approaches such as Tier 1 and Tier 2. Perhaps you could combine wholesaling and Tier 3 rehabbing. At this point a student might say, "Yes, that Tier 3 sounds good, but I do not have the money to purchase the house." As I said, you do not need the money to purchase the house.

There are other people that will do it for you. Then you might say, "Yes, that sounds great, but I do not have the money to rehab it." Well, that is okay too. There are also avenues to fund renovations as well. With proper support and mentoring to teach you how to move forward in your business and to acquire the right resources to grow, you too will learn to implement the best strategies to become a successful and prosperous real estate investor.

So, do you need money to get started or not? Everybody says, "Yes. I need at least some money, probably a fair amount of it." However, that is not always the truth. In many situations, investors do not need money because we can control properties without it.

I encourage you to think hard about the blindness that you might be living under. This is a false idea that you need money to start your business. You need to just start. This will eliminate 80% of the fears associated with getting your business off the ground and becoming a profitable real estate investor.

The money is there. The resources are there. You just need to make a decision.

This would be a great time to discuss cash purchases versus finance purchases. In many cases, we make offers called a "Cash Offer." Other times, we have offers designated, "Offers Contingent on Financing." The difference is that financed purchases are created in conjunction with a local bank that is agreeing to finance you based on your work history, your tax returns, paycheck stubs and your credit score.

If those elements are favorable to you, then you should absolutely work with locally based banks. Interest rates will be anywhere from four to five-and-a-half percent depending on the current economic indexes. Working through a bank in your area is the cheapest money you will ever borrow, and it is the easiest money that you will ever borrow when it comes to the best returns on your investments.

Unfortunately, some people persist in saying things such as, "Yes Zack, but I cannot pull that off. I do not have a job." Or perhaps, "I do not have tax returns, and my credit is below 640." In this situation, you should focus on becoming a cash buyer. Those same people may say, "What, me a cash buyer?"

Yes, that is what I said. You just need to know where to acquire the money, and how to get the resources. Banks are not in the business of conducting cash purchases. Banks specialize in finance purchases. Other lending institutions will allow you, the investor, to operate cash purchases.

These organizations change the game for someone like yourself who is trying to invest in real estate. For some people, it is challenging just getting started, especially if they do not have the resources or the credit. Fortunately, other lending institutions will still fund your real estate investing venture.

Let us say you aim to conduct a Tier 3 investing plan. In this case, you will be a cash investor. Nevertheless, you will be able to utilize asset-based lenders to fund your purchase and, in some cases, your remodel fees as well. The beauty is that you are truly stepping into real estate investing where you can leverage your financial literacy of utilizing 'Other Peoples' Money' to make your own money.

You have probably heard of OPM which stands for Other Peoples' Money. This is the greatest thing I ever learned from my real estate investing coach. He showed me how I was confined to the wholesaling level because I had this misconception that just because I did not have great credit or access to substantial amounts of money, I could not progress to more lucrative strategies.

I believed I had to keep wholesaling because anything else was beyond my means. Now do not get me wrong here. Wholesaling is great. You can quickly make $5,000, $10,000, $15,000 on each deal. I previously told you a story about a 10-day wholesaling project that netted $8,000, but the real money is made when you rise to Tier 3 acquisitions.

With a Tier 3 game plan, you can work deals producing $20,000, $30,000, $40,000, even $50,000. The last three fix and flip deals I conducted cleared over $50,000 within a 30-day period!

You can see that the money is in a Tier 3 fix and flip program, but too many people are blinded by fears or misconceptions or lack of knowledge, and will not grow into the Tier 3 level. They have the misunderstanding that they do not have money because they have told themselves that over and over again. "I do not have money. I cannot do this. I do not have a good credit score. I cannot do this."

Sadly, they have lied to themselves constantly, but the truth is far different. The reality is that if you want move into a Tier 3 investing strategy, you can get access to funds from an "asset-based lender."

There are different lending options out there for you to utilize. One is obviously a finance type lender which is usually a local, community type bank. You could even work through a big-box bank, but I would encourage you to search out community banks or credit union banks within your area first.

They generally have less restricted guidelines for funding, and have a much more personable working relationship with you. These local banks can really help you get favorable loans.

Another types of funders are the asset-based lenders, also known as "hard money lenders." These financiers only care about the deal. They do not really care about you personally. They do not care about your credit or your job.

They do not even care if you have a job. Their sole interest is if you can acquire a deal that is less than 70% of the ARV (After Repair Value). Their interest has little to do with the purchase price and that is a big difference. Institutional type finance lenders advance you capital based on purchase price; therefore, if you are buying a property for $100,000 and they want you to put 15% down, then they are financing you $85,000 of the purchase price.

Where the asset-based lender differs is that they look at the After Repair Value. You might be buying a property for $100,000 but once it is fixed up, it is worth $200,000. They base their loan off of the future fixed-up value. If they say, "We will loan you 70% of the ARV," and the ARV is $200,000, that means that they will advance you up to $140,000 to purchase that property.

Their investment is safe. They know you are going to make money. If you acquired it under contract for $100,000, they will fund the entire

$100,000 for you. Now you have bought the property using a cash investing institution such as an asset-based lender or hard money lender.

The beauty is that no money out of your pocket is needed! Sure, these lenders do charge you a lot more interest than a normal brick and mortar type community bank, but it is money that you did not have. As long as you run your numbers correctly; adding in your fees to this asset-based lender, you are still making $20,000 or $30,000!

Does it even matter what they charge as an interest rate? No, it does not.

Do not be blinded by their interest rate. If they are charging you 12% interest, it is not something you should be worried about at all. Pay them whatever they want as long as you can still get the deal and make a profit.

There is also what we refer to as Bridge Funders. These Bridge Funders are people who will loan you $20,000 to $30,000 for home remodel and renovation work. That is another piece of how you are able to structure a Tier 3 deal without using any of your own money.

So, again, the question is if you need money or not. It depends on your chosen strategy. The best advice my coach taught me was to not let my lack of knowledge stop me from growing.

I did need to educate myself, but I also needed to move forward and not stay static. That is how I want to encourage you as well. I would not be where I am today if it was not for a coach who pointed me towards the things I now know.

ROB STANFIELD

"Zack - You are AWSEOME! I love ya man!

I thought this was going to be a long, drawn-out journey, but with your guidance this year (2017) in 6 meetings, I have built a Portfolio of seven single-family properties, and one multi-family unit. These two deals are making me $70,000/year passively!

I could not have done this without you. You have simplified the process, and ensured my safety with my investments to a point that I am comfortable. You paved the road so I could see a better plan for my future, and the future of my family.

My COCR is incredible at 74.1% on the seven houses, and 32% on the multi-family.

I am on target to retire in two years, and live off of my passive income! That could be moved up to summer of 2018 as we still have seven months left in 2017, and we are closing on a package deal every 60 days!

You have taught me how to negotiate, and get what I want out of a deal.

I would recommend ANYONE from any level in their business to work with you. I had no knowledge before I met you, and no portfolio. I only had a dream and you helped turn that dream into a reality!

Thank you for everything!"

- Rob Stanfield

CHAPTER 9

FINDING YOUR BUYERS

"Do not let what you cannot do interfere with what you can do." - John Wooden

This chapter really should be called, "How you get paid" because this is the process through which you close the deal resulting in the buyer compensating you. Whether that is an investor buyer, a retail buyer, or a tenant buyer; this is the finale of the whole process from choosing your strategies to identifying the right areas and finding the right deals to researching and contracting the property.

Remember, you can do all those steps perfectly but it is all a waste if you cannot execute on the close. To do so requires having the right buyer for that specific deal.

Throughout the entire process, you need to keep the exit in mind. Never wait until later to build your buyer's list or acquire your potential exit for that right buyer. From the get-go, you should be looking for the right buyers to match with your properties. As you begin to execute your strategy, keep the end result in view.

Going in to each new deal, ask yourself if this is a Tier 1 wholesale which will require a cash buyer? Is it a Tier 2 creative financing model which will require a tenant buyer? Is it a Tier 3 rehab requiring you to identify a retail buyer? Perhaps you are pursuing a Tier 4 which will ultimately require a renter to occupy the property?

Mapping this out up front will allow the best tactic for selling your deals quickly and simply. It is crucial for real estate investors to plan ahead so you do not get stuck trying to figure out how you are going to sell, lease, rent the house, or merely sell the contract.

It is frustrating to put so much work into a deal and not have the right person ready to take the property. You do not want excess inventory sitting around without a buyer or renter. Therefore, I encourage you to spend some time considering how you can market for seller leads while you are marketing for buyer leads.

You ultimately want to bring the two together to close the deal. The type of marketing campaign you settle on will be dependent upon which tier model you have used for the particular properties being considered.

For example, if Tier 1 was your approach in this specific instance and you are aiming towards wholesaling, assigning, or selling the contract for the property, 90% of the time you are going to need a cash buyer.

This way, you can sell the contract to a cash buyer who also covers your assignment fee while paying ready money for the property. In this situation, you need to identify and cultivate a potential cash buyer.

Clearly, you will need to know where cash buyers live and how to connect with them. Generally, cash buyers are looking for two types of properties: rental properties or fix-and-flip properties.

They can pay cash up front and rent it out themselves or fix and flip properties that they want to invest in using a cash payment. There are resources to help identify those areas wherein potential buyers of this type might be found.

For instance, you can go down and do title searches on properties that are being closed in specific areas. This allows you to see if various properties have a mortgage on them. If not, then you know that someone paid cash for that property.

Subsequently, you can mail that property owner and let them know that you are interested in a potential deal that would fit their criteria for purchasing.

You can also find cash buyers at local auctions whether at the court house or a private auction company. Cash buyer leads can also turn up at your local Real Estate Investors Association.

Alternatively, other ways to find cash buyers could be through software techniques. Strategies such as these allowed me to get up and started very quickly in my business. My coach also pushed me into finding and identifying the markets in which cash buyers were found.

With a little forethought, I developed my game plan to target economically dynamic markets or neighborhoods where cash buyers were active. I deployed a marketing campaign in those neighborhoods to target deals for those active buyers. I learned to keep the end result in mind as I moved forward.

In the Tier 2 creative financing model, you are going after properties that you can control through some type of seller financing. Most of these properties you can obtain through a simple process known as a "Sandwich Lease Option." A Sandwich Lease Option allows you to put a long-term lease on a property with an option to purchase at a later date.

This gives you the ability to find a tenant buyer for the property that will pay you more than the agreed monthly rent. Thus, you get monthly cash flow off that property, and a potential buyer with strong intent to purchase at a later date as well.

When you are acquiring tenant buyers, you can find them through mortgage companies. These could be people who did not qualify to get a loan but they still desire to be a homeowner. You can also find tenant buyers through property management companies.

Again, these potential buyers want to be involved in home ownership, but for whatever reason, have not had the ability to get a loan from a bank. Lastly, you can find tenant buyers through rental properties. Those who are renting houses in a particular area, and would love to own a home in the neighborhood but do not have the ability to get the proper loans.

These are all qualified tenant buyers for you to reach through a marketing campaign. This campaign can take the form of a direct mailing campaign or running ads to acquire a list. As you build a list of potential clients, you have a stream of ready and eager buyers when you close the deal that meets their needs. No overhead inventory; you have buyers ready to step into your properties.

Now the Tier 3 client is your fix and flip type buyer. In this case, you are working with a retail buyer. There is really no need for you to build a marketing plan or spend money on acquiring first-time home buyers when there are agents that you can work with. This is all they do.

They are called buyer agents. Buyer agents specifically work with people who are looking to buy a property. With the Tier 3 plan, once we have acquired the real model and are fixing it up to go back on the market, we simply turn the marketing over to an agent and allow them to list it. That is their special skill set - bringing a retail buyer to the property. Simply done. No other work is needed from us. We outsource through an agent to list the property.

Lastly, the Tier 4 purchaser aims to buy and hold. In this buy and hold situation, our buyer is actually a renter. Someone who is going to rent that property, and pay you a monthly rent payment.

You will make cash flow off that property monthly. Now Tier 4 is different than Tier 2 because in Tier 4, you own the asset. In the previous creative financing model, you do not own the property. You simply control the asset.

With Tier 4, our end goal is to find a renter. You could self-manage this marketing campaign efficiently by running your own ads on the paper or on Craigslist. You may put signs out in the yard of the property to find your tenant.

Furthermore, to qualify a potential client and put them in your unit, you could outsource the process simply enough. Hiring a property management company will take the burden of minor details off your shoulders so you can focus on your next deal and not be the manager.

This is what a property management company does. They deal with the daily specifics. They market for tenants all the time. They have a list of prospects to rent your unit or house. I strongly encourage you to outsource that aspect as well. Find a property management company to manage your real estate portfolio.

Always bear in mind, buyers or renters are your exit component in the whole process. With Tiers 1 and 2, you will be doing your own marketing and finding your buyers. You will be building a relationship with those investors who paid cash as well as those tenant buyers looking to attain homeownership through a strategy you put together through creative financing.

Just keep in mind that you are constantly working on your buyer's list if you aiming at Tier 1 or Tier 2 strategy investments. Never stop marketing for these buyers.

One of the most important processes for a Tier 1 or Tier 2 investor is to effectively market for those types of buyers. You must stay engaged in the marketing and communication for these buyers.

Follow the scripts and the processes to acquiring good, qualified buyers into your business model so that you do not have to worry about finding a tenant buyer or a cash buyer when you get a property under contract. It is a simple process of understanding that these buyers are out there.

They are looking for great deals, and you can find these deals for them. You have the knowledge and tools to research and analyze the deal to make sure that the property or the specifications meet the qualifications for your tenant or cash buyer.

On the other hand, Tiers 3 and 4 can be outsourced to a management company or a real estate agent. Utilize their skill sets to put a tenant in your property or find you a retail buyer to buy your fix and flip property.

DAVID RALL & DONNA GILBRETH

"After teaching and studying real estate, I thought there was nothing else I needed to learn. I realized very quickly that I was wrong after I attended one of Zack's live workshops. While I had a lot of pieces, I didn't put them together with the Zack glue until going to one of his classes.

I saw the workshop advertised and thought, 'oh, it's just another seminar' but something told me I should go. Zack had a system that he provided that I did not hear from anyone else. He does more than provide training. He actually does it too.

We saw this as the express train to what we wanted to do, rather than having a ten-year plan. Our biggest goal was to get the systems in place, and have automation in place. It worked! It's a proven system that works!

Zack was able to take concepts and tweak it for what we needed to provide a custom coaching package for us. We did not have to go through training that wasn't relevant to our needs. This is going to double our business in the next six months.

One of the challenges we faced was with funding for the type of deals that we wanted to get into. Zack got on the phone, and helped us out.

In the last 60 days, we have gone from nothing to $2.7 million on the books. We have also closed five deals in the past 60 days, and made almost $200,000. We have three in negotiations, six under contract, and seven that are currently waiting to be sold.

The best part about working with Zack is that he is always available when we need him. He has a fantastic infrastructure setup, and a wonderful support staff.

Zack will save you a lifetime by starting from day one. If you want to get there quicker and be on the leading edge of your business, you are going to need a mentor and a coach. If you are going to succeed in this business, you are going to need a person like Zack to help you.

Zack and his team are dialed in. That is why we stay with them!   *David Rall & Donna Gilbreth*

CHAPTER 10

CLOSING THE DEAL AND GETTING PAID

"The wise young man or wage earner of today invests his money in real estate." –Andrew Carnegie

Things may be going very well along the way, but something comes up late in the process. Remember, the deal is never over until a check is in hand. You must stay with the transaction to the very end if you want to make a profit.

Finding a buyer does not seal the deal nor does getting a property under contract. The matter only ends once you have received a check in hand and the deal closes. Be clear on that point so you will not get 90% through the process only to falter at the end.

Stay committed to the deal until the end. Stay committed to the paperwork and the footwork all the way through to closing. Bear in mind that these deals can easily slip or fall through the cracks even at the very end if you are not careful.

It is especially important to make sure all your paperwork is signed by the seller and the buyer, tenant buyer, or the cash buyer. Paperwork is an easy thing to overlook, but vitally important for a solid close.

Another crucial piece to start building upon is your power team. These are all the people you are going need on your team to make sure that your business is successful and maturing. Skilled people like a handyman, a contractor, a title company or a real estate attorney if your state requires one to do the closing.

This is the team you want to assemble to support the growth of your real estate investment business. It is paramount to build a relationship with these people and build a relationship of mutual understanding.

Your team needs to share your vision and understand your aims and procedures. Likewise, you need to understand how they operate or their processes for closing a deal.

You should familiarize yourself with how the closing attorney or title company you are working with closes transactions. What are their standard procedures; what will they expect from you; what should you expect from them?

Get an idea of how long it generally takes them to close or run title searches. Once you have a feel for the timing involved, you will not get discouraged if the deal does not close when you think it should. Make sure you stick with the process until the end so that you can get paid.

Ultimately, the worst thing that can happen is for you to check out too soon after doing so much footwork up front. Be aware, deals do not always close like they are supposed to, but you cannot get dispirited.

Here is a current example of a deal I am working through. I will make somewhere around

$130,000 once everything is in the books. This deal was supposed to have closed two weeks ago, but little obstacles kept popping up.

My buyer is aiming to secure a VA loan, but VA loan processes are much different than normal loans. FHA standard loan processes are extremely particular about what they want fixed.

For example, they would not close or fund escrow because a set of stairs in the garage going up to a loft did not have a handrail on the last flight of steps. I had to go fix that.

Similarly, they did not like the fact that one of the facial boards had a crack which might allow weather to seep into the attic. I had to oversee that fix too. There are often little things that not even an inspector would catch; however, this VA inspector who came out to look at the property noticed.

These were minor things to handle but it pushed our closing back. If I would have pulled out of that deal and went about my other business and not worried about it, this deal could have fallen through. You have to prepare to stick it out because deals falter for all types of reasons.

Occasionally, a situation arises because of an error or oversight by the lender. Once a lender did not proof the buyer's financial statements until the very end of the process. Then they made an issue out of it and delayed the whole transaction.

You would think that since they had 30 days to get all this together, the paperwork would be in order, but it was not. They pushed this simple process to the very end instead of acting on the paperwork early in the procedure. If you are closing through a title company or an attorney, stay in communication with them every couple of days especially towards the end of the procedure.

Just a short email to ask how everything is going. "Do I need to do anything?" "Have we gotten any feedback?" "Has anything popped up that would stop this from closing on time?" Be proactive!

Communication is key in the closing process. Stay in the deal until the very end. This preparation will save you time and headaches. With this VA buyer I was telling you about, I was prepared for this closing to drag out because I was involved.

I knew that things were coming up, and I was fixing them quickly. However, we still had to schedule a second inspection three to four days out. Be prepared for the process to drag out.

Let's say that I am wholesaling a deal and my cash buyer is bringing asset-based funding to the table. Well, if I only have two days left on that contract as agreed upon by me and the seller, but the buyer needs seven days to get his funds into escrow, that is a significant challenge. You have to go back to the seller and let them know that you need an extension for closing.

Let me walk you through some types of closings. A wholesale payday closing is one of the easier closings to accomplish. You are assigning the contract to the cash buyer, and now it is their responsibility to close either through escrow or not.

Nonetheless, for you to close on it efficiently, make sure that your cash buyer has enough time to close based on the agreement that you have made with the seller. Also, there is one document that must be in place. It is called the Assignment Agreement. That is your closing document. That is the certificate between you and the cash buyer so that you can get paid and the cash buyer can move to escrow.

Another type of closing is a retail house payday. A retail house payday uses an agent. This representative finds you a buyer and brings the buyer to the table in which case you must make sure that this buyer has opened escrow, has submitted an earnest money deposit check, and is abiding by the inspection period and contingencies.

Make sure you supply all the requests from the buyer and if they come back with a repair list at the end of inspection period, you will need to negotiate that into the final agreement. They might come back to you with 20 things they want you to adjust but you are not entitled to do all 20 things.

You are responsible to fix any safety or hazard issues, but other little things like light bulbs are not your responsibility. You can negotiate a repairs list, but once it is agreed upon, you will need to handle whatever repairs you approved before closing.

You will also need to make sure that the bank or the asset lenders you have used to buy that house will settle the payoff amount due at the closing office, the escrow office, title or an attorney's office. Believe it or not, that has been an issue before.

Make sure the various agencies involved are communicating with the buyer's lender and that funding is in process. Check to see that closing documents are being taken care of and a hard disclosure statement is being presented to you so that you can check all the fees and requirements associated with that closing.

As you can see, you need to stay in the deal but eventually, you will show up at escrow, sign your paperwork, collect your check and move on to the next deal.

One more type of closing that I want you to be aware of involves a tenant buyer. I am talking about a Tier 2 strategy where you have allowed a tenant to move into a sandwich lease option deal. Likely, you have agreed on a term for them to get approved for funding to close.

Ultimately, since with this strategy you do not own the asset, you might have to do a transactional close. Through this you use transactional funding to purchase the property from the seller before turning around to sell the property to the tenant buyer, typically within the same day.

Another approach uses a form called a DOF form. I teach this method constantly in our live real estate training events. Once you learn DOF forms, there are multiple ways to close transactions.

Closing the deal is by far the most important aspect of what we are doing. It was one of the things that I had to hire a coach to teach me about so I could guarantee my safety in closing transactions. I also encourage you to find out about one of our live real estate investor events. I teach seminars several times a year.

I will walk you through deals. We will walk through marketing, and we will walk through closing. In three days, my team and I can help you get your business up and running very quickly. I refer to this as jump starting your real estate investing. You are seeking information, you are educating yourself at a live event, and you are getting some hands-on guidance at my events.

A key step towards your success is attending one of my live events. You will learn from me and my team so that you can start implementing the processes that are required and experience a hands-on learning approach.

Become involved, learn the various steps and the processes from me that you need to do to excel. You will gain experience by going to find deals and bringing them back into the event. We will then work on those deals together so that you can see how quickly a payday can arrive. I encourage you to find out more about this right now.

VIVA WILLIAMS

"I actually had a friend share with me what Zack was doing, and he was so excited explaining what Zack was doing.

I went to a three-day class that Zack had, and I knew this was something that I had to do. I was very motivated and encouraged that this is something that I should do.

My biggest challenge is procrastination. Having a coach definitely keeps me accountable, keeps me on track, and keeps me organized. That has helped me tremendously.

I considered coaching also because I know myself, and I know that I won't stick with it if I don't have that motivation or I feel too frustrated to move forward.

I would tell anyone that if I can do it, you can do it too. It is priceless information within Zack's teaching. The fact that I can call him and his staff anytime I need them, that in itself is amazing."   *Viva Williams*

CHAPTER 11

WHAT TYPE OF MONEY CAN YOU MAKE?

"Buying real estate is not only the best way, the quickest way, the safest way, but the only way to become wealthy." –Marshall Field

This is the chapter that will take your real estate investing business to the next level. This is your action chapter! I want you to believe in yourself, and I want you to believe in this process. I have built a team to help you grow and get to the next level.

If you can accept the help that is being offered, my team can assist you in reaching the financial security that you are seeking. Ask yourself, "where am I financially? What about my retirement plan? Where will I be in 10 years if I keep doing what I am doing right now?"

Do you have a plan that you are going to execute in the next two years that will allow you to retire? Perhaps you are trying to find your niche alone and are faltering. Do you feel like you're banging your head against a wall?

The worst thing you can do is do this alone. Where will you get guidance? Who can you bounce ideas off of? Not having someone that knows where you are trying to go, a mentor that can give you the answers and the resources to build your business with you, is a lonely and frustrating place.

Is your current place in life where you want to be? If not, what do you picture an ideal life to look like? How quickly do you want to get there? Trying to learn real estate investing alone will take you years, if you even stick with it.

However, with the right help and support and a game plan specifically designed for you, your efforts will catapult you into success. Where do you want to be in the next 12 to 24 months? I can promise you that your expectations are probably very realistic, but you need to change your mindset.

If you become open-minded, if you become coachable and believe in a process that has worked over and over again and allow yourself to accept the help to get you where you want to be, the sky is the limit!

So many people want to be successful but they do not know how to be successful. Those people break into two different categories. There are those people who say, "I will just do it on my own. I will just figure it out myself."

They will spend the next two, three, or eight years trying to figure this out or they will get themselves into bad investments. I have people who hire me to be their coach all the time, and we find out immediately that they tried to do it on their own, got into bad investments and they have lost money. Only then do they realize they needed guidance. I do not want you to make that mistake.

The money that you lose on a bad deal is money you could have invested in yourself to be a better real estate investor to succeed much faster. Think about it from time invested to the time to succeed. The best investment I will ever make in myself is investing in my education.

There is a second group of new real estate investors that say, "I do not want to do this alone. I am coachable, and I do want to invest in myself. I do want to learn from those who have gone on before me and been successful."

These are the real estate investors that find success much faster. They are open-minded, they are open to information, they are open to being pushed and they are open to being coached. I certainly hope you are in this crowd.

At this point, you could do nothing, which is an option. You could try to do it alone which I do not recommend, or you could do it with my team.

If you allow my team and I to help you succeed, you could easily be earning $200,000 to $300,000 a year. If you started this method on a part-time basis conducting two or three Tier 1 deals a quarter, you may net an extra $30,000 a quarter. That puts you well above $100,000 a year just working the Tier 1 method.

If you only accomplished one Tier 3 deal per quarter, with an average profit of $25,000 per flip. This puts you at $100,000 a year! If you only do Tier 1 and Tier 3 deals part time, you are potentially earning $200,000 a year as a real estate investor.

That is a remarkable business model! We can then reinvest into your portfolio properties and start buying rental properties. You could be living off your rental income, and meanwhile allow your business to keep generating $200,000, $300,000 or $400,000 a year!

You just need to have the right guidance. You just need to have the right input and knowledge to know how to build this business model. I can help you. Do not do this alone. It is the worst mistake you will ever make. Invest in yourself, gain this knowledge and believe in the process by which you can make it happen.

Some of the best investors I have ever met knew the power of getting help. They were successful, but knew that they had to do whatever it took to get the assistance they needed to grow their business.

I want to leave you with a gift today. My gift is three strategy sessions where you can talk to one of my Student Advisors or my Business Advisors about where you are in your business, and where you want to go. What strategy is best for you and what type of a game plan do you want to achieve?

I really want to help guide you down a process of getting you to where you want to be in real estate investing.

So, I encourage you, take me up on this free gift. Be part of our team and let us help you excel as a real estate investor. We have helped hundreds of people do exactly what you are considering, and I am sure we can help you achieve the success that you desire.

Take my free gift and use it to the fullest. Get three free strategy sessions from one of my Student Advisors and let us help build your business in the right direction so that you can have the lifestyle that you have always wanted.

Until we meet at one of my live events or I get to speak on the phone with you in person, I wish you the best and I wish you success. I only hope that you will take action today. If you do not take action or reach out for assistance, you will never receive it.

Take me up on my free gift. It is yours. Utilize it, get on the phone with a Student Advisor and let us build a plan that will work for you. This is Zack Childress and I will see you soon.

Your Mentor,
Zack Childress

Claim Your Free

One-on-One Strategy Session Here:

www.REISuccessAcademy.com/bonus

Or Call and Request your Free Strategy Session at:
707-310-8113

TIMI ABNEY

I met Timi after she had been through a couple coaching programs and several bus tours with other coaches. She was, by far, the most skeptical student I have ever met face-to-face, but I saw a lot of motivation and determination within her.

So, I challenged her. I challenged her to come to just one of my events, and I told her if she wasn't impressed, then I would not coach her any further. At that event, she asked so many questions. I know she was testing me. I answered every one of them. At the end of those three days, she asked me to be her mentor. With a smile on my face, I accepted.

Timi is now one of my most successful students, and my biggest fan. She went from a stay-at-home mom to the biggest investor in her market. She also has her own REIA where she teaches others in her area how to invest, and work with other investors. She is also on my workshop team of experts that meet with each student that comes to my three-day training.

This is what it is all about. Relationships, growth, reaching your goals and dreams, and helping other people.

I teach the 5F Lifestyle. Faith, Family, Freedom, Fitness, and Fellowship. This is what I have built my life around, and this is what I want you to open up your mind to so that you can create that balance in your life just like I have, and just like all of my successful students have.

Don't forget your free bonus. It's on the next page. Let's get your life right. Give us a call today and let us help you like we have so many others.

Here's Your
FREE BONUS
($497 Value)

**Claim Your Free One-on-One
Strategy Session Here:**

REISuccessAcademy.com/bonus

or

Call and Request your Free
Strategy Session at:
707-310-8113

Made in the USA
San Bernardino, CA
08 May 2018